FLORIDA'S ABANDONED BOATS

THOMAS KENNING

AMERICA THROUGH TIME®
ADDING COLOR TO AMERICAN HISTORY

America Through time is an imprint of Fonthill Media LLC
www.through-time.com
office@through-time.com

Published by Arcadia Publishing by arrangement with Fonthill Media LLC
For all general information, please contact Arcadia Publishing:
Telephone: 843-853-2070
Fax: 843-853-0044
E-mail: sales@arcadiapublishing.com
For customer service and orders:
Toll-Free 1-888-313-2665

www.arcadiapublishing.com

First published 2022

ISBN 978-1-63499-404-0

Typeset in Trade Gothic 10pt on 15pt
Printed and bound in England

CONTENTS

ABOUT THE AUTHOR

THOMAS KENNING is an author, educator, and adventurer. He holds a MA in history from American University in Washington, DC, and teaches the subject in St. Petersburg, Florida. As a writer and photographer, he is passionate about documenting the vibrant history and stunning ecosystems of the Sunshine State.

INTRODUCTION:

A YEAR OF DERELICT BOATS ON AND UNDER THE WATER IN FLORIDA

The story of Florida's motley fleet of derelict boats—abandoned and forlorn—is, somewhat counterintuitively, a story about people. After all, an abandoned *anything* begs the questions: What happened here? Where did all the people go? These captainless, crewless craft, adrift and rudderless in Florida's balmy waters, tell a story of identity in crisis—a story about the mismatch between who we want to be and who we actually are, as individuals and as a state-wide community.

In a materialistic society like ours, what you own and what you don't—what is within your grasp and what is not—is wrapped up inextricably with who you are and how you present yourself to the world. We are all players in this game of projection. Sometimes we win, sometimes we lose, and sometimes what we thought we had firmly in hand drifts away on a receding tide.

Case in point: A few years ago, I bought myself a kayak. It was the kind of thing that no one else could have known that I wanted, a total break with my humble origins as a landlocked Midwesterner, enamored of the kind of outdoor recreation that kept my two feet in full contact with the firmest of ground. But that plucky little boat changed my life. It gave me a truly native perspective on the adopted Florida home which I have come to love. To put it another way, seated atop my kayak, I was transformed into a true Floridian. No turning back. No asterisk. Self-proclaimed and in the eyes of my neighbors and the law—it's official now.

Perhaps more than any other state, Florida is defined by its water. With a mean elevation of 100 feet above sea level and longest coastline of any state, the line between land and water is often at best a marshy blur. On my kayak, I explored many of its 700 freshwater springs. I paddled deep into the mangroves, until the sky overhead disappeared, and I could no longer swing my paddle freely with ease.

I dashed daringly across open shipping lanes just to get to the other side. More than once, enchanted by the natural splendor around me, I lost track of time only to find myself on the wrong side of an outgoing tide.

My kayak has been a passport into Florida's blueways, natural Florida at its most pristine. Florida at its most serene, I thought.

And while this ideal turned out to be mostly true, my kayak also offered inadvertent entry into the Sunshine State's largest *de facto* junkyard—a semi-aquatic trash heap uncontained.

Florida. A land full of flowers indeed—after a sort. Colorful. Eye-catching. Always in season.

Everywhere you look, around every leisurely bend in the shoreline and behind every verdant stand of mangroves was an omnipresent tableau of discord: A bonnethead shark and a half-filled soda bottle. A cormorant trailing a tangled length of ghost line. A manatee surfacing amidst the floating shards of a shattered plastic cooler. An airborne mullet, majestic and bold, bellyflopping into one of the Gulf Coast's annual red tide blooms. An oyster bed serving as the final resting place for a forlorn boat, reeking of spilt fuel and the festering stench of black mold.

I read once that an accident of the prevailing currents sweeps a lot of Florida's marine litter out to sea, depositing it on faraway shores. Maybe that's true. But if this is what's left—if this is the result of Mother Nature cleaning up after her untidy children, I have to ask—my god, what are we doing to this state for which we profess so much love?

I wonder how many people up on shore—cruising along the expressway, choosing the right club for the 18th hole, kicking back under the covers with the AC on, living their lives, doing other Florida things—have any idea what it's like out here in the quiet inlets and bays, where the well-intentioned beach clean-ups can't reach, where the most conscientious and civic-minded of our neighbors can't mask the true extent of our human mess.

Over the last couple of years, paddling has become a big part of my life. I rearranged a lot in order to get out on the water more and more frequently. Mid-morning in the middle of the week, Florida's waters started to feel like my native realm. You could say I was beginning to take some ownership. I was able to grab the occasional bottle or candy wrapper, to clean up here and there on the margins.

But even if I quit my day job entirely, there was no way I could tackle Florida's massive trash problem on my own. For starters, I'm one man in a kayak. Second, the problem is a collective one. Another orphan scrap of plastic washed down the drain. Nobody's mess and everybody's.

A reactionary response wasn't going to cut it. Rather, it is necessary to proactively stem the flow of litter at its source. And that was going to require a communal awareness of the true extent of the problem.

So, I grabbed my camera and started to document the waste that was beyond my ability to remove. That way, I could at least bear witness to the most dramatic offenders in the overturned wastebasket that has spilled over onto Florida's gorgeous shores.

Thus, I present to you, dear reader, this humble book. A document which isn't intended to glorify or profit from our environmental woes, so much as to edify and reveal this phenomenon—to portray it in the glaring light of the Sunshine State.

These are Florida's derelict boats—raw, uncut, *in situ*—garnished with miscellany refuse on the periphery of the paradise that we call home.

THE GRATEFUL DAD
GULPORT

1

AN UNSYMPATHETIC SEA

Florida has seen its fair share of gnarly shipwrecks—the kind that go down not just beneath the waves but in the history books. The kind that inspire treasure hunters and those whose hulls make for epic artificial reefs.

For example, many of the first recorded encounters between Europeans and Florida's native peoples came as a result of shipwreck, when an errant storm or an unseen shoal caused some slavers' ship to wash up on Florida's sandy shore. Sometimes the survivors joined Calusa or Tocobaga society, other times they were themselves enslaved, and still other times, only an array of flotsam survived to bear witness to their frothy fate.

In the days before advanced satellite and radar technology gave plenty of warning ahead of a brewing hurricane, major storms caught many a vessel unawares. Typical were the *Atocha* and the *Santa Margarita*, part of a twenty-seven ship Spanish convoy in 1622. These ships took an estimated $250 million in colonial plunder to the shallow bottom off the Keys.

Two centuries later, in 1827, the HMS *Nimble* and the *Guerrero*, a Spanish ship smuggling more than 500 chained Africans into slavery, were engaged in a running gun battle; both ships ended up floundering on a reef in the Florida Straits. More than forty Africans drowned, likely still bound below deck as the crew of the *Guerrero* abandoned ship.

In 1980, the gargantuan M/V *Summit Venture* collided with Tampa Bay's Sunshine Skyway Bridge, sheering away a section of the bridge's southbound span, killing thirty-five motorists when the roadway dropped off beneath their vehicles.

Those show-stopping calamities—plentiful across a half century of accumulated incidence, but rare in the day-to-day scheme of things—are worthy of our memory.

For sure, they warrant the many volumes of historical writing that they have inspired over the centuries. But the most common shipwrecks littering Florida's coast are much smaller.

They are a steady tide consisting of thousands of lesser tragedies, personal in scale, playing out simultaneously from the Atlantic Coast to the Gulf Shores, hundreds of times in the average year. Theirs is a story of overreach, of a sinking middle class, of an idealized version of the success slipping quietly under the lapping waves of an unsympathetic sea.

Let's paddle around in these waters for minute. I think you'll see what I mean.

THE GRATEFUL DAD
GULPORT FL

2

A LIFE ALL ITS OWN

What happens to the boat that becomes unmoored in a surging storm? What happens to a dream when the money runs out? What happens to a status symbol when it is run down by the wheel of fortune?

If any of that happens in tepid waters of Florida, the answer is most often predictable. One and all, they end up trapped amidst the spider legs of mangroves or on some anonymous shoal.

Gone, out of reach, but not forgotten, because a derelict boat has a life all its own, even if its owner has written it off as dead and gone.

nderin'
at
a Gorda

3

A DREAM UNDERWATER

To my eyes, an abandoned boat is a curious thing, evocative of a unique spectrum of sentiments. These forsaken vessels are as alluring as they are lurid. A well-maintained boat—one that is shipshape and Bristol fashion—is emblematic of hope, leisure, and conspicuous consumption. On the other hand, a derelict boat—one run up on a sandbar, taking on water, listing, left for dead—is a jarring symbol of exposed disappointment. It is the aspirational American dream underwater, a calamity of changing fortunes, of an overly optimistic man from the middle class misjudging his prospects and biting off more than he can chew. It is the hubris of Icarus writ small, with shades of Odysseus and Poseidon.

It is a kitchen table tragedy worthy of Arthur Miller. Or Norman Lear, at least—dripping with rivulets of distilled schadenfreude, tempered with a sobering hint of "There but for the grace of God, go I."

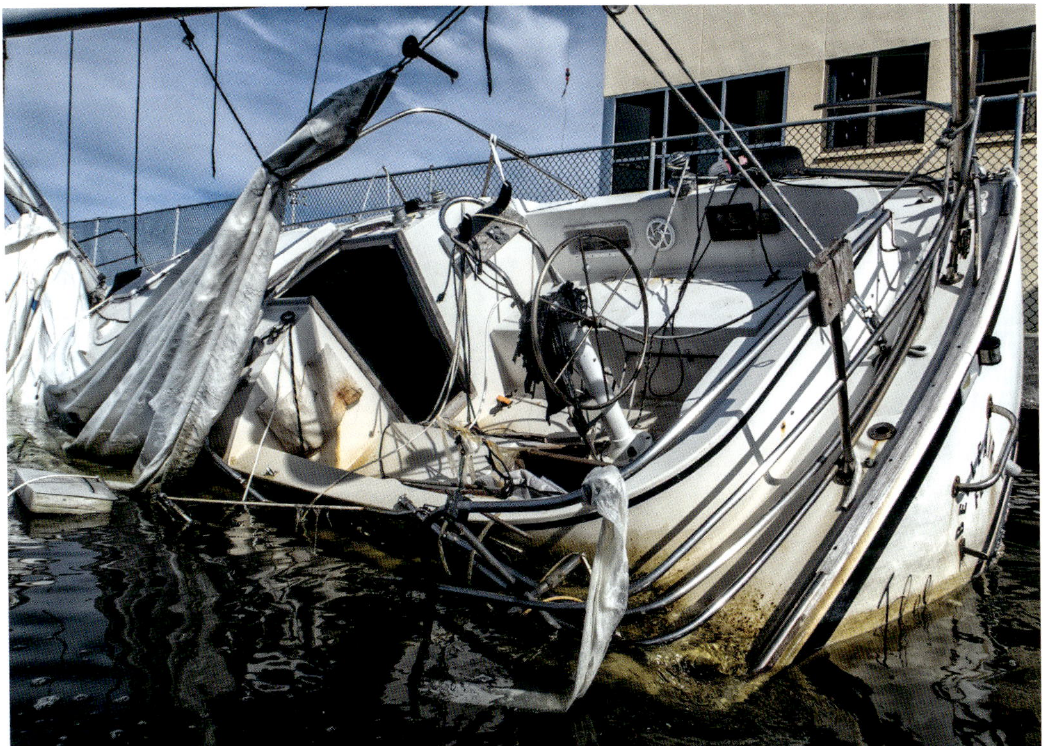

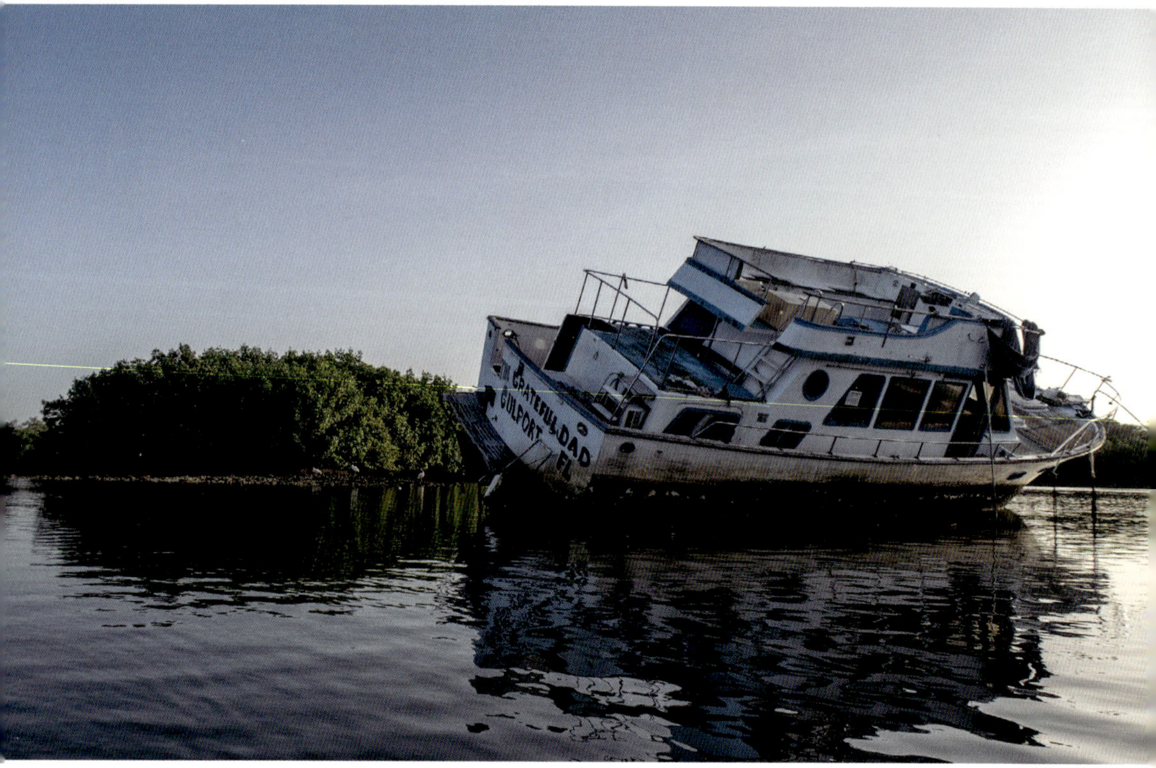
GRATEFUL DAD
GULPORT FL

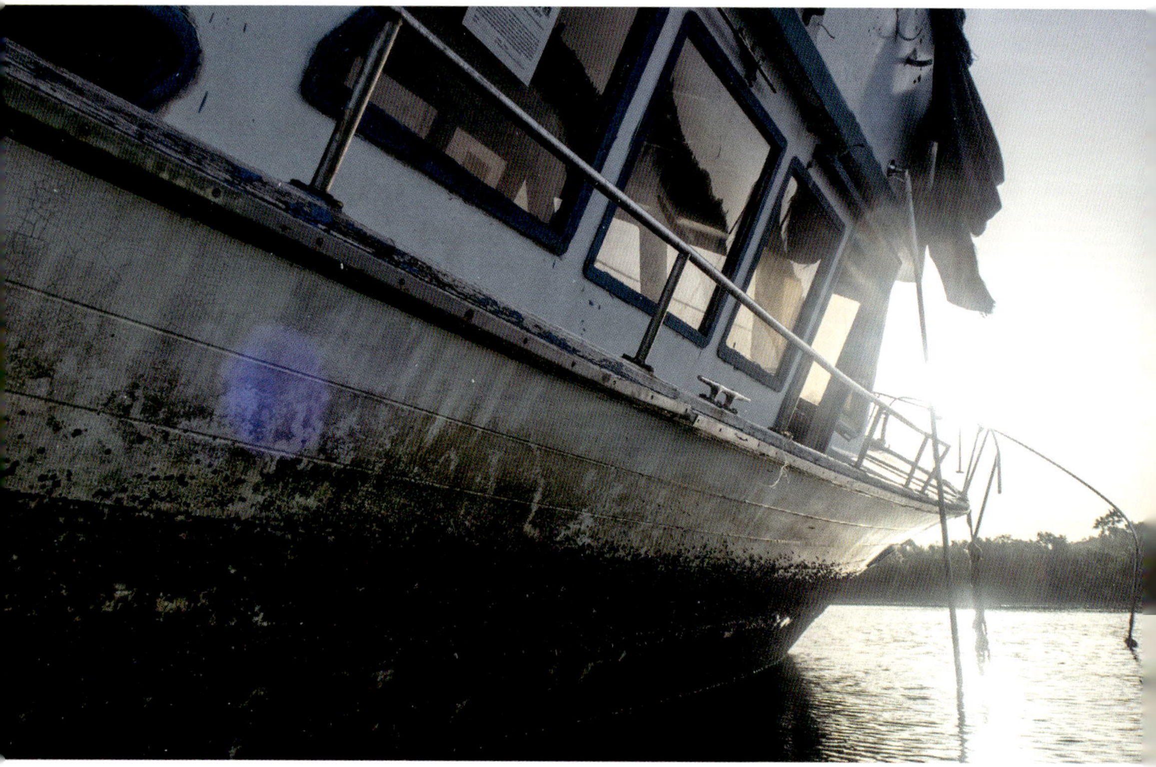

4

UNFLATTERING FACTS

ar and away, there are more boats registered in Florida than any other state. By most calculations, the Sunshine State accounts for just under 10% of all recreational boats licensed in the nation, with more than 900,000 active registrations in 2020.[1]

Something like three quarters of boats belong to households earning less than $100,000 a year, explaining, perhaps, why such a relatively large number of them fall into disrepair. Depending on your lifestyle, that's a comfortable enough budget for most folks. But if something goes horribly awry with your vessel, it's understandable that there may be little other opinion, financially speaking, than to just let it go.

Personally, I can't afford a boat—to berth it, fuel it, maintain it. Or, when the time comes, to dispose of it with care. It's beyond my own humble means. The same could be said of the erstwhile owners of many of the boats featured in these pages. The main difference is that I already knew this about myself. Others, it would seem, had to learn this unflattering fact about themselves the hard way.

5

GOOD TASTE

The largest, most luxurious craft are the ones likeliest to be sanctified with a nickname beyond the impersonal alphanumeric code, the registry numbers doled out by the state's bureaucracy like "now serving … " tickets at the deli counter. There is something poignant about the snappy, self-assured tone of a boat's name, when that name is plastered in lilting script on the side of a craft that itself is pitched at a sickly angle *vis-à-vis* the horizon, gulping water as if it had gills. So often these maritime monikers are formed from upbeat puns—a reference to the good life, perhaps, or having the wind at one's back. A nod to possibilities as wide open as the distant horizon. Their authors were self-confident men and women, christening a very visible symbol of having made it in life, proclaiming their optimism and worthiness for everyone on the sea and shore to see.

The names of these ruined craft read like an indictment from the gods, a litany of hubris and other crimes against humility and good taste:

Aquaholic
Sea Senora
Row V. Wave
Ships n' Giggles
Bacon in the Sun
She Got the House

Some are in on joke, or at least willing to tempt fate:

Unsinkable II
Future Poor Person

Most of these quips aren't exactly clever, even when the men and women who did an internet search for "cool boat names" think they are. But that is hardly the point. The boat to which they are attached says, "I don't need to be funnier than you—I'm already winning life with a score much higher than yours. The jokey name on the side of my boat? It's not really for you. Rather, it's *on you*."

And it's true. I can read the name of your boat, I can groan at the hoariness of your wordplay, but in the end, you can't hear my toothless mockery because you've already set sail. Or you're roaring away under the power of some dual outboard rig that costs as much as my house, and I am left standing with the plebs on shore.

But the boat shoe is on the other foot now that your vessel has run aground.

Meant to broadcast success in tall, boldface letters, the name on a derelict boat is recontextualized, hinting instead at hardships and disappointments that were unthinkable in earlier, headier times. An abandoned boat reeks of loss. Its sinking, a kind of very public fall from grace.

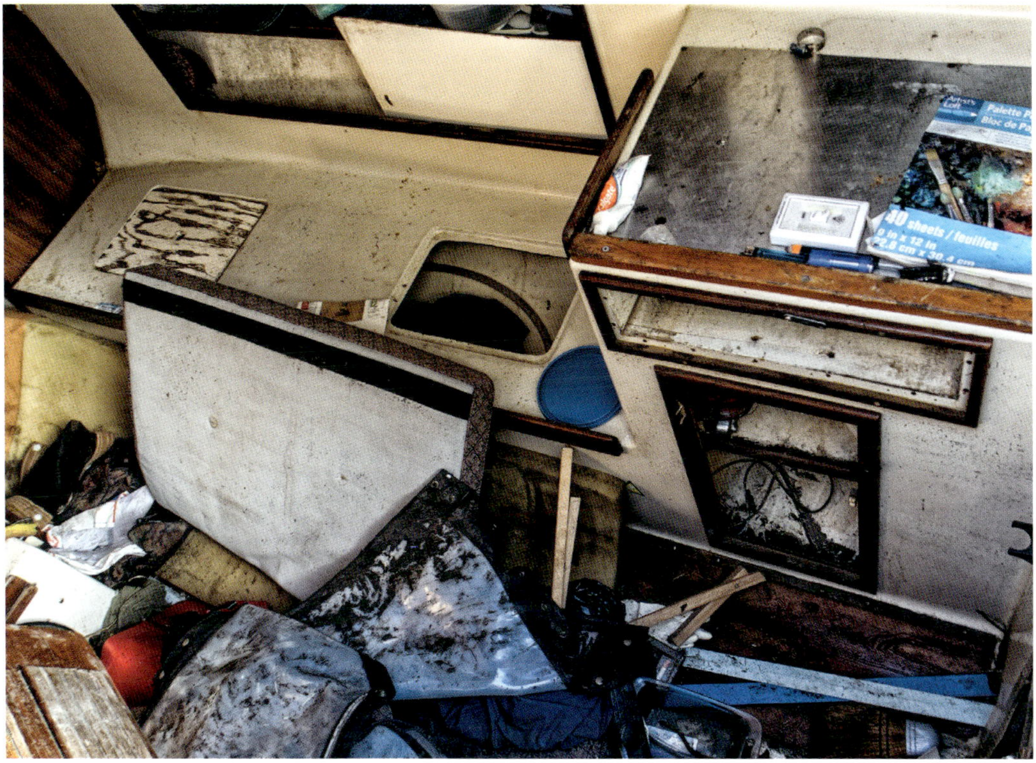
40 sheets / feuilles
9 in x 12 in
22.8 cm x 30.4 cm

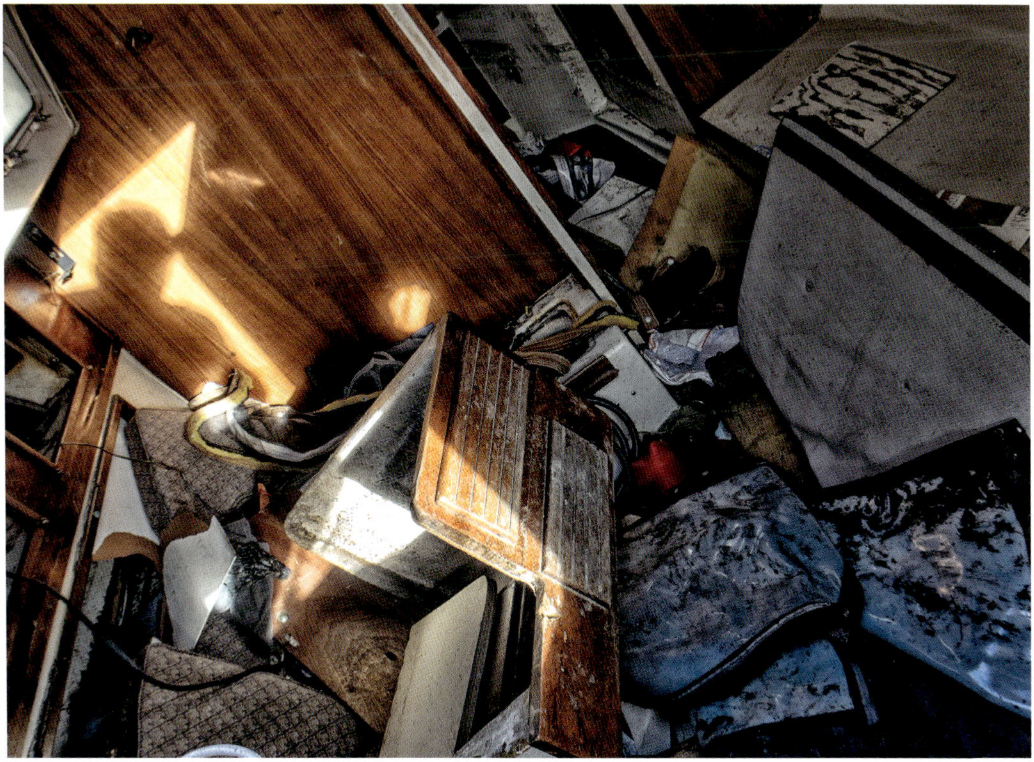

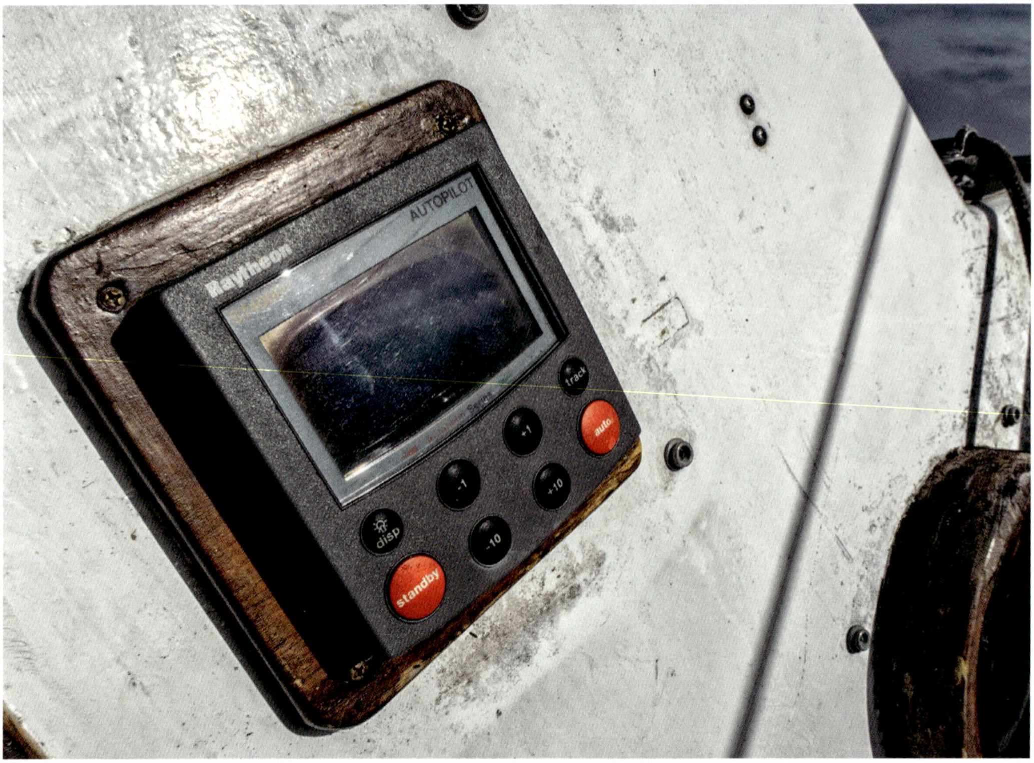
Raytheon
AUTOPILOT
track
auto
+1
-1
+10
-10
disp
standby

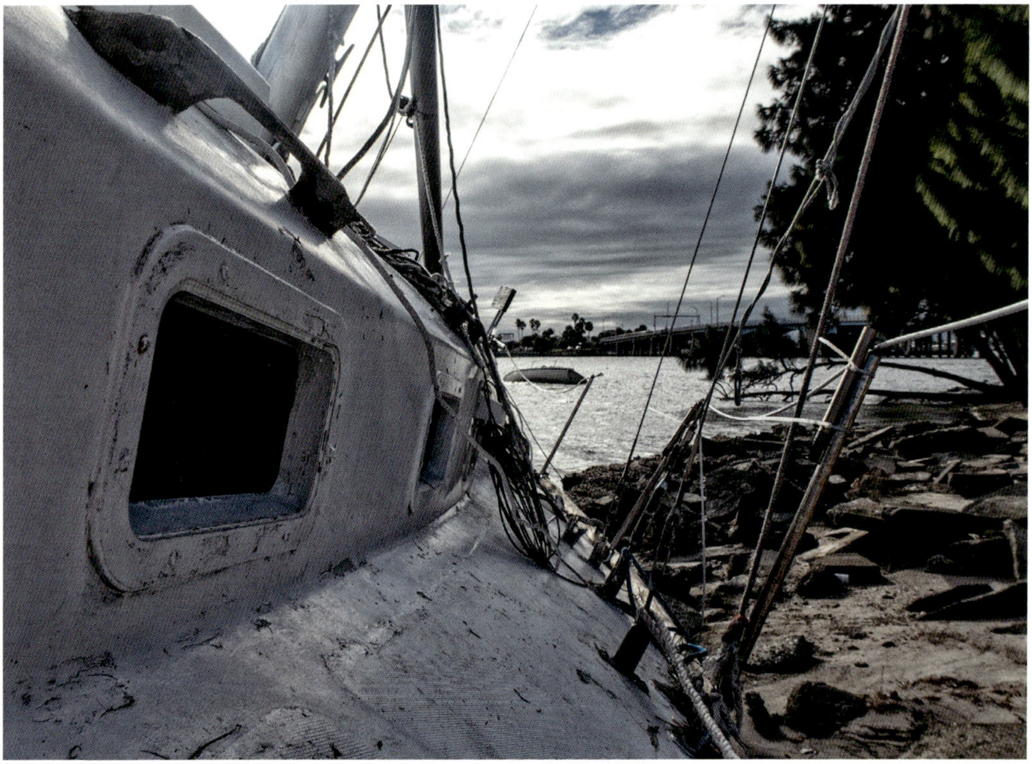

6

ESCAPE FROM REALITY

In these wrecked boats is written both the privilege and the disparity of our times. Boat ownership sits at the crossroads of the polarized demographics of modern America, breaking sharply along racial lines. According to industry statistics, boat ownership is an overwhelmingly white pursuit. If the figures of the States Organization for Boating Access are accurate, in the 2010s, nearly 18% of non-Hispanic whites owned at least one recreational boat, compared to less than 5% ownership in either the African American or Hispanic communities. It's estimated that whites own 87% of all boats in the United States.[2]

Crunching the numbers yet another way: In Florida and elsewhere, white men's boats float away nearly as fast as people of color buy them, in terms of raw numbers.

The open water, it would seem, is a pretty racially homogenous place. This might, in part, explain the rise of another primarily white pastime: the much-ballyhooed phenomenon of pro-Trump boat parades—Trumptillas, they were dubbed—during the 2020 election cycle.

In a *Tampa Bay Times* story published on September 17 of that year, the owner of a boat prominently flying a "Trump: No More Bulls--t" flag explained to a reporter that he "would never wear a Trump shirt or display a bumper sticker or yard sign at home."[3] The piece, which examined the apparent popularity of Trump among Florida's boaters, continued:

> The water, however, is "neutral ground" where, he said, you can fly your Trump flag and "you don't have to fear for your business. You don't have to fear for your neighborhood."
>
> [The boat's owner], lounging in his Pabst Blue Ribbon swim trunks, said repeatedly his flag is not so much about "loving Trump," the man, specifically. He talked instead

about wanting to signal the things he's against, laying out grievances with Black Lives Matter, the media and liberal "movements."

The sea provides a refuge from the constraints of polite society. It is the last safe place where a man can deny systemic racism without having to get into a whole conversation about the facts. The last place he can pretend that the world isn't changing around him.

So, when I see a wrecked boat, there's a whole raft-load of sociopolitical symbolism and subtext, too—in the right light it can look like an old order of things, fraying at its edges, enduring but not eternal. Another true believer who won't make it to the parade's rallying point.

But these aren't entirely new observations. Boating has always been about escape.

7

YACHT ROCK

onsider, if you will, the genre of music retroactively dubbed "yacht rock." Popular between about 1975 to 1985, this special brand of upbeat, melodic soft rock was defined by artists like Christopher Cross, Rupert Holmes, Jimmy Buffett, Captain & Tennille, Steely Dan, and Hall & Oates.

Its Doobie bounce sounds good on a clear sunny day. It usually has a dry, clear studio sound, held up by a buoyant electric piano line. Its grooves, such as they are, are laced with lyrics that are wry like the names painted on the hulls of the very yachts from which it so often blasts. Those lyrics often tell tales of heartbroken, foolish men, seeking to escape from the travails of ordinary life—yearning to live a simpler life, unburdened by the responsibilities of the office, of a dreary love life, or of politics.

Cultural critic Steven Orlofsky has summed it up, writing that both in its original context and now, yacht rock represents "a defiant, fingers-planted-firmly-within-ears disregard of any and all political unrest."[4]

Yacht rock is almost exclusively written for and by white males of a certain socioeconomic status; to the extent that this music, featured on its own seasonal Sirius XM station, has an audience, it looks a lot like the people who own boats.

And on that note, just why is it that the recreational boat is so clearly gendered in American culture as masculine, alongside hunting rifles, sports cars, and the decidedly non-yacht rock of Van Halen? Specific rates of ownership among men versus women aren't clear, but a quick visual survey the next time you are out on the water will reveal that its men most often at the helm. While there are plenty of women out on the water, it's rare to see many parties made up entirely of women. On the other hand, there are plenty of boys-only groups to be seen, whether they are fishing or simply cruising.

In a society where so many spaces, from gyms to bars, have been stripped of any strong gender coding, it would seem that on the high seas at least, the patriarchy is still afloat.

8

ZOMBIE BOATS ON RAZORBLADE SHELLS

My favorite time to make photos of derelict boats is at low tide—when keels are exposed unnaturally to the air, appearing like turtles overturned and vulnerable. It's then that the plight of these lost boats seems most dire and dramatic. It's then that it seems most impossible to imagine that these boats might ever float again—indeed, that they ever could float at all.

Wait a few hours, though, and many of them will. As the tide rushes back in, and the oysters open their razorblade shells, most of these slumbering behemoths will list wearily back to life. Zombie boats, neither dead nor alive, going nowhere and doing no one any good.

Let's hope their former skippers are faring better since the separation.

9

THE MOST HARMFUL WRECKS

Derelict boats pose a threat to the environment around them. You can smell it in the air when you're downwind. You can see it in the rainbow slick across the water's surface.

They are dead in the water, lifeless but not inert, like the hundreds of manatees struck each year by Florida's active boaters. Except Florida's orphaned boats carry on, wreaking havoc like some fleet of zombie mariners. They leak noxious chemicals—fuel and lubricant that do neither the fish nor the dolphins any good. Tides and currents push them into mangroves, smashing the trees' spidery limbs. Tossed about this way, they grind oyster beds under their keels.

But the most harmful wrecks do all this and more—they are hazards to navigation for the seaworthy craft still plying the channels. They are icebergs in balmy waters, lurking just below the surface—vipers ready to strike when your guard is relaxed. Lying in wait to pull other boats down to their low level, they are bullies.

Taking this photo, my kayak was swept up on the incoming tide. An exposed screw, glistening, galvanized steel—barnacled, sure, but gnarly as ever—tore into the thin hull of my craft. I had to shove off using my paddle, and once I was free, I couldn't deny the disheartening flow of a slow leak in the bow of my trusty vessel, the perch from which most every photo in this collection was shot. I limped back to my launch point, stopping occasionally on the leeward side of a stand of mangroves to bail my crippled craft.

She's certainly no motorboat. She's no grand sailing ship. But damn it if the combination of a patch and stubborn force of will hasn't kept my kayak afloat. Which is more than can be said for so many other ostensibly grander vessels brought low by the wear and tear of Florida's blueways.

Left long enough, that husk of a boat may become a *de facto* oyster reef or the toehold for an especially hardy red mangrove propagule. This is a small comfort, but Florida's waters—as overfished, algae-bloomed, and generally abused as they are—are deserving of an occasional silver lining.

10

A FOR ABANDONED

The decal used by law enforcement officers to mark a derelict vessel is a kind of scarlet letter—a safety orange *A for abandoned*. It is a fate at least as shameful as being condemned as an adulterer. Both labels bear a whiff of betrayal, but at least the sin of adultery implies passion and a lust for life. Abandonment is an act of impotence—a failure to thrive.

Florida's Fish and Wildlife Conservation Commission (FWC), in cooperation with local law enforcement, monitors derelict vessels along the state's 1,350-mile coastline. The agency maintains an online database marking the location and status of every reported vessel. Around 500 pins can be found on the interactive map at any given time, but some officials guess that the actual number of derelict boats could be three times as large.

As of 2016, Florida code grants law enforcement officers the power to fine the owner of any vessel at risk of becoming derelict, a condition legally defined as:

1. The vessel is taking on or has taken on water without an effective means to dewater.
2. Spaces on the vessel that are designed to be enclosed are incapable of being sealed off or remain open to the elements for extended periods of time.
3. The vessel has broken loose or is in danger of breaking loose from its anchor.
4. The vessel is left or stored aground unattended in such a state that would prevent the vessel from getting underway, is listing due to water intrusion, or is sunk or partially sunk.
5. The vessel does not have an effective means of propulsion for safe navigation within 72 hours after the vessel owner or operator receives telephonic or written notice, which may be provided by facsimile, electronic mail, or other electronic means,

stating such from an officer, and the vessel owner or operator is unable to provide a receipt, proof of purchase, or other documentation of having ordered necessary parts for vessel repair.[5]

In Florida, salvaging the wreck of a boat to which you don't hold the title is considered theft—subject to criminal charges—no matter how long the wreck has rested inert in public waters. If you or I wished to claim a damaged vessel—to put in the work to reclaim and restore it—we would first need to initiate and finance an investigation through the FWC or another law enforcement agency.

If I see a vessel that I believe is abandoned, how do I make claim to it and start the claims process?

The first requirement is to report it to a law enforcement agency. The law enforcement agency will collect a fee for beginning an investigation, conduct an investigation under Section 705.103, Florida Statutes, and determine the owner of the vessel. If the vessel is not claimed in the process of the investigation, the law enforcement agency may allow the transfer to the finder with evidence of the investigation and a copy of the Lost or Abandoned Property Certificate FWCDLE-003. The finder would then make application to the Florida Department of Highway Safety and Motor Vehicles (DHSMV) to have the title put into his name.

The investigation process usually takes between 45 days to 120 days or longer. The cost associated with the investigation is usually between $300 and $600. The costs may be more or less than this depending on the investigation requirements.[6]

In any event, unlike a junked car, a wrecked boat holds little value. There just isn't much of a market for 27 feet of sun-bleached fiberglass and sodden wood.

A truly wrecked boat is mostly headed to one of two places—straight to the bottom or straight to the dump.

11

AN END OF LIFE FOR EVERY VESSEL

State law once required permits from the Florida Department of Environmental Protection and United States Army Corps of Engineers for the removal of any derelict craft. While this provision was meant to ensure that all salvage operations were compliant with environmental best practices, it also represented yet another unnavigable sandbar between the owner of a faltering vessel and that vessel's proper disposal.

In an effort to encourage higher rates of compliance, the state legislature waived this requirement in 2013. The incidence of abandoned craft in Florida's waters have only increased since that time—it would seem the greatest barrier to responsible removal of derelict craft is related neither to the permits involved nor the modest expectation that salvage meet a baseline level of environmental safety. Rather, the hardest part of removing a craft that is dead in the water, is removing a craft that is dead in the water.

The cost of removing such a vessel is around $400 per foot but can reach as high as $50,000 per vessel depending on just how solvent the craft is. This expense is far too often assumed in large part by the public after a period of due process ends with the inability of the vessel's owner to repair or remove it.[7]

If the government does assume the cost of removal, the boat's legal owner will be barred from registering another vehicle, trailer, or vessel in the state of Florida until such time as their debt is paid off.[8]

As the FWC so lyrically puts it, in what turns out to be a profound meditation of a faceless bureaucratic agency on the inevitable mortality of us all:

Every vessel owner should realize that there will be an end of life for their vessel. If they have an opportunity to legally sell the vessel near its end of life, that's great! If not, the owner must have a plan to properly dispose of the vessel.

Illegal methods of disposing of your vessel:

- Sinking as an artificial reef or Fishing attractant without DEP and Corp of Army Engineers approval and permitting. This is Felony Dumping (Jail Time).
- Discarding by cutting it loose and letting it drift away hoping it will disappear. This is Felony Dumping (Jail Time).
- Pulling it up to a boat ramp and grounding it and leaving it.
- Mooring it without any plan to continue its upkeep and maintenance.
- Burning the vessel in open water to destroy it.
- Giving it to someone who says they will take it off of your hands without properly transferring title and ownership.

You as the owner are responsible for removing the vessel from the waters of the state and having it transported to an approved landfill for destruction. The cost for doing this is a fraction of what the costs are to remove it from the water and destroy it after it sinks. Do your part to help the environment, the safety of others and the welfare of the state by disposing of your vessel responsibly.

Intentionally dumping your vessel on the waters of the state is a 3rd degree Felony punishable by up to 5 years in prison and/or a $5,000.00 fine. Also, restitution to the state for the later cost of removal, fines, community service, probation or parole, lost registration privileges, and continued litigation for repayment in full. If you can't do it by yourself, find someone who can help you. Don't take a chance of getting into serious trouble.[9]

So, consider yourself fairly warned.

It's pretty stern language, and I don't blame the FWC for not mincing words. But clearly these legal sanctions haven't really gotten to the heart of the issue—Florida's waters are still littered of orphaned craft. Based on the comparatively paltry number of prosecutions under the severest of these laws, it seems like intent is either hard to demonstrate or not the primary factor driving the crisis.

The fact is, if the luckless owner of this wrecked boat could afford to pay a fine or the fees associated with its removal by the state or any other party, his or her boat probably wouldn't have ended up adrift or underwater in the first place. The Florida statutes discussed here are, in part, talking about the criminalization of poverty—the punishment of those without the financial wherewithal to clean up their own mess. For those who *can* pay, law firms around the state advertise their specialty in mitigating the penalties assessed to clients who run afoul of these regulations. Either way, it seems unlikely that these laws are in any meaningful way effective in deterring the dereliction of boats or in recouping the costs of removal.

With that in mind, it might be more helpful to view the problem from a structural perspective. The derelict boat epidemic is a failure of the market and a failure of the state to properly assess the lifetime cost of owning, operating, and disposing of a boat—and to then spread that cost out over the whole period of boat ownership.

12

THE RISING TIDE

Abandoned boats abound, and not just after storms like Irma and Michael, when their numbers spike.

In the scheme of things, there are greater human-fueled problems than Florida's bumper crop of derelict vessels—from the red tide that now regularly washes up on shore to our increasingly overdrawn aquifer which we are depleting faster than it can refresh, just to name a couple.

But there are implications to all of this—implications that speak to something even deeper than a swamped sailboat lying at the bottom of a previously-navigable channel.

In truth, the problem of a derelict boat seems to be only a very visible representation of deeper societal ills, of the ways in which we are failing each other and the ways that the system is failing so many of us. Derelict boats are, among other things, a problem of financial literacy—of understanding just how much boat one can afford, including the upkeep. It is the intersection of our ailing educational system and our inability to differentiate between wants and needs in a capitalist society hell-bent on breaking down that distinction.

We play with our toys and throw them away when they break with little sense that this cavalier attitude has any impact larger than ourselves and that we have any obligation to clean up after ourselves. But it's more that.

The ghost fleet of derelict boats dotting Florida's coast is symptomatic of a system that reduces every barrier to acquisition but fails to properly assess the value of sustainability. Our inability to match the cost of removal to the revenue generated by licensing and penalties is testament to, among other things, a failure of leadership—an inability or unwillingness on the part of elected officials to govern responsibly.

Celebrating our freedom to do without ever pausing to consider the ripples and rings we might make in the calm waters around us. But this is a textbook economics question.

Our leaders are running a perpetual sale on the cost of licensing boats here in Florida, giving little thought to what happens after our toys break. Instead, the mantra is buy now, pay later (or never). Affordable financing, Memorial Day boat show, tax holiday, ten percent off, minimal fees. In Florida, we can all live like princes—happily ever after. Except, that is just an adman's come on. The pitch of "Have your cake and eat it too," fails to account for what happens to the plastic spoon and paper plate.

One proposal being bandied about in Tallahassee is to mandate insurance on all watercraft in the state, similar to what is already legally required of automobiles. These policies could be made to cover recovery and disposal of derelict craft, thereby spreading these high costs across all policy holders and the entire life of their vessels, mitigating the financial burden placed on the public. Policy premiums would surely raise barriers to entry for would-be boaters whose bank accounts are not fully above water—but that might not be a bad thing.

Fewer boats on the water probably means fewer would go derelict in the first place, especially if insurance companies assessed the risk of ensuring prospective clients and their specific craft before issuing or renewing policies. Those boats that remained afloat would be more likely to do so, because the insurance company would have a vested interest in verifying that such craft meet basic standards of maintenance and safety.

I'm not an actuary or a policy wonk. Maybe this isn't the most effective way to address the issue. All the same, GEICO doesn't want to be anywhere near your rusty bucket of a motorboat—just like a car that isn't street legal, stricter rules about insurance might mean that your leaky dingy would have to stay parked in the driveway.

Everyone should have an opportunity to enjoy the outdoors. Everyone deserves a chance to get out on the water. But does everyone need a boat all their own? A boat that sits at anchor or tied to the pier six days out of seven, tying up resources and draining bank accounts?

Boat sharing clubs offer another compelling path toward more sustainable access to the water, easier on the Earth because we need fewer boats to meet our common demand and easier on the wallet at the same time. And no one dues-paying member would be on the hook for end-of-life costs associated with vessels as they age out of the club's fleet. But it's even more than that still.

Derelict boats are just one manifestation of the problem of downward mobility—the stagnant wages of the middle and lower class in the face of ever-rising costs of living. Any way you look at it, the American middle class is shrinking. For so many reasons, the United States is becoming a nation of haves and have-nots, of rich or poor with fewer and fewer in between. According to the Pew Research Center, "From 1971 to 2019, the share of adults in the upper-income tier increased from 14% to 20%. Meanwhile, the share in the lower-income tier increased from 25% to 29%." While that isn't all bad news—some previously middle-class folks are definitely winning—the median income of those in the upper class is accelerating away from the largely stagnant incomes of the middle and lower classes.[10]

The rising tide of our economy is clearly not lifting all boats.

WATER
120 140 160 220
50 70 100 c
TEMP
120 140 160 220 F
50 60 70 100 c
TEMP

13

OUR SUNSHINE SOCIETY

Who are we as a society—with such grand aspirations to the high life, so susceptible to the fantasy that we might all partake—when a whole phantom fleet of derelict boats argue the opposite point?

Wherever we find this orphaned trash, we find a most unflattering reflection of ourselves.

There surely are bigger problems facing Florida than a few thousand boats gone astray. But those boats point to a whole mess of bigger problems beating down on our Sunshine society—among them, unsustainable consumption, rising inequality, and an inability or unwillingness to reckon with the finite resources of our planet. Add to that list, for good measure, a dubious belief that the government which governs least is always and in every case the best.

The overgrown barnacles on the keel of an abandoned boat could just as easily represent the blemishes on a battered American dream. The truth is and always has been that some of us ride up on deck, the sea breeze in our hair. The rest of us—we're just hanging on for dear life, skimming by, only rarely above water from cradle to grave.

It seems like we owe our neighbors—human, animal, or plant—a little more than that. We're together in the same boat after all. Let's make sure it's one that floats.

ENDNOTES

1. Basic Facts of Recreational Vessel Population and Recreational Boating Demographics." *National Marine Manufacturers Association*, 2015, https://www.obcc.org/?page_id=306

2. Bohnsack, Brian and Aiken, Richard. "Demographic Influences on Changes in Boat Ownership and Boating Related Recreation." *States Organization for Boating Access*, 2013, http://www.sobaus.org/membersonly/2013conference/tuesday/Brian-Bohnsack_General-Session.pdf, Accessed January 9, 2020.

3. Spata, Christopher and Contorno, Steve. "Does Donald Trump own the ocean?" *Tampa Bay Times*. September 17, 2020, https://www.tampabay.com/life-culture/2020/09/17/does-donald-trump-own-the-ocean/

4. Orlofsky, Steven. "In defense of yacht rock." *The Week*. June 15, 2019. https://theweek.com/articles/847297/defense-yacht-rock

5. "Abandoned Vessel Claims Process FAQs." *Florida Fish and Wildlife Conservation Commission*, 2021. https://myfwc.com/boating/waterway/derelict-vessels/

6. "Derelict, Abandoned & At Risk Vessels." *Florida Fish and Wildlife Conservation Commission*, 2021. https://myfwc.com/boating/waterway/derelict-vessels/claims-process-faqs/

7. Taylor, Janelle Irwin. "Lawmakers grapple with what to do about abandoned boats." *Florida Politics*. January 28, 2020. https://floridapolitics.com/archives/317261-lawmakers-grapple-with-what-to-do-about-abandoned-boats

8. Pinkard, Carrie. "Do NOT Abandon Ship: How Derelict Vessels Are Clogging Florida's Waterways." *WUSF*. August 12, 2019. https://wusfnews.wusf.usf.edu/news/2019-08-12/do-not-abandon-ship-how-derelict-vessels-are-clogging-floridas-waterways

9. "Abandoned Vessels." *Florida Fish and Wildlife Conservation Commission,* 2021. https://myfwc.com/boating/waterway/derelict-vessels/abandoned-vessels/

10. Horowitz, Juliana Menasce, Igielnik, Ruth, and Kocchar, Rakesh. "Trends in income and wealth inequality." *Pew Research Center.* January 9, 2020. https://www.pewsocialtrends.org/2020/01/09/trends-in-income-and-wealth-inequality/